The 2000s

Stephen Feinstein

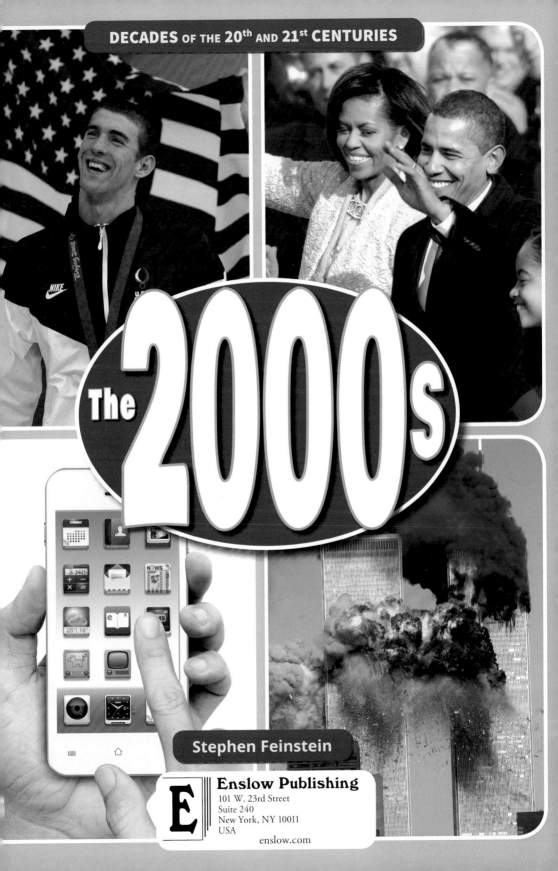

The 2000s

Stephen Feinstein

Enslow Publishing

101 W. 23rd Street
Suite 240
New York, NY 10011
USA

enslow.com

Published in 2016 by Enslow Publishing, LLC.
101 W. 23rd Street, Suite 240, New York, NY 10011

Library of Congress Cataloging-in-Publication Data

Feinstein, Stephen.
The 2000s / Stephen Feinstein.
    pages cm. — (Decades of the 20th and 21st centuries)
Includes bibliographical references and index.
Summary: "Discusses the decade 2000-2009 in the United States in terms of culture, art, science, and politics"— Provided by publisher.
Audience: Grade 9 to 12.
ISBN 978-0-7660-6939-8
1. United States—Civilization—1945—Juvenile literature. 2. United States—Politics and government—2001-2009—Juvenile literature. 3. Two thousands (Decade)—Juvenile literature. I. Title.
E169.12.F4477 2015
973.931—dc23

2015010952

Printed in the United States of America

To Our Readers: We have done our best to make sure all Web sites in this book were active and appropriate when we went to press. However, the author and the publisher have no control over and assume no liability for the material available on those Web sites or on any Web sites they may link to. Any comments or suggestions can be sent by e-mail to customerservice@enslow.com.

Contents

Introduction

As the United States entered the decade of the 2000s, Americans looked forward to a time of peace and prosperity. They had every reason to feel optimistic. After all, the world had survived the Y2K transition without the slightest hint of the widely predicted disaster—when computers around the world would supposedly go haywire and disrupt every aspect of life dependent on technology.

The 1990s under the presidency of Bill Clinton had been a time of relative prosperity for many Americans, and there was low unemployment. The Internet was quickly taking over many aspects of life as people increasingly went online to communicate with others, conduct business, and shop. People even used the Internet for entertainment. Many new businesses were formed to facilitate the functioning of the Internet and to provide various services. Many of these technology companies went public and sold stock to people wishing to invest in the latest and coolest great idea. Indeed, by the late 1990s, it truly seemed possible to get rich quick. The period became known as the dot-com boom.

At the end of the decade of the 1990s, people expected the good times to continue. Sadly, it was not long before the party was over. By March 2000, it became apparent that many of the new dot-com companies were failing and filing for bankruptcy. Suddenly the dot-com boom was widely recognized for the bubble it was. Stock prices would fall dramatically over the next couple of years. First the new dot-coms crashed, followed by the older established technology companies and then all sorts of businesses. Unfortunately, the dot-com bust would lead to a recession, and many would lose their jobs.

Then came that tragic day. A horrific event occurred on September 11, 2001, that shocked all Americans, as well as much of the rest of the world. Members of an Islamic terrorist group known as al-Qaeda hijacked four passenger planes and crashed them, which killed about three thousand people and injured many thousands more.

Fear and panic spread throughout the nation. Never before had Americans felt so vulnerable. Five days later, on September 16, President George Bush declared a war on terror. For the rest of the decade and beyond, the United States would be at war—first in Afghanistan, where al-Qaeda leader Osama bin Laden was believed to be hiding, then in Iraq, where its president, Saddam Hussein, was thought to be developing weapons of mass destruction (WMDs).

Also high on the government's list of priorities was ensuring the security of the nation. The Patriot Act, signed into law on October 26th, 2001, gave law enforcement agencies the right to spy on anyone without a court order. A huge new bureaucracy, the Department of Homeland Security, was established to detect and respond to terrorist attacks.

By the middle of the decade, the economy had begun to revive. The stock market, at least in certain sectors, recovered from its losses. And the housing market seemed to go wild as home prices shot up. People began to speculate in houses, just as they had previously done with stocks. It became easy to get a mortgage to buy a house. Banks were willing to loan money to anyone who could put a mark on a lending application whether or not they would be able to pay back the loan. But just like the dot-com bubble, the housing market bubble would soon burst, which almost destroyed the entire financial system and the nation's economy. The housing market crash began in August 2007, and home prices would continue to fall throughout the following two years. Meanwhile, in October 2007, the decade's second stock market crash began, and the market would not hit bottom until March 2009. America was now in the midst of the worst financial disaster since the Great Depression of the 1930s. In 2009, America's newly elected first African American president, Barack Obama, would have to act quickly to prevent the Great Recession from turning into another Great Depression. He was successful, but millions of Americans lost their jobs, and millions more lost their homes.

So as it turned out, the decade of the 2000s, which started out with great promise, became a time of great troubles.

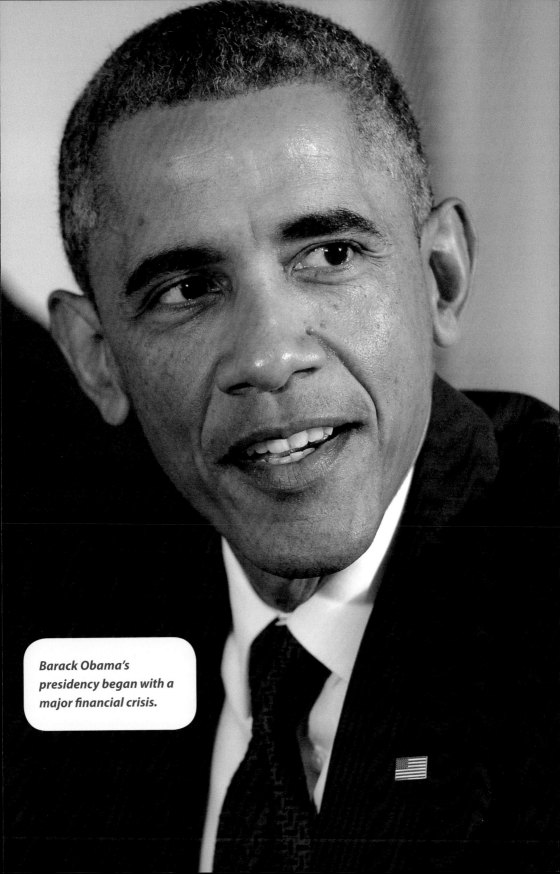

Barack Obama's presidency began with a major financial crisis.

Pop Culture, Lifestyles, and Fashion

Early in the decade, events occurred in America with an impact that would be felt throughout the rest of the 2000s. These would affect the way Americans lived and thought about themselves and the world.

A Day Americans Will Never Forget

Tuesday, September 11, 2001, began no differently than any other weekday. It was a beautiful morning in New York City with the sun shining in a clear blue sky. People in the streets of lower Manhattan were on their way to work. Many employees in the 110-story Twin Towers of the World Trade Center were already at their desks.

At 8:46 A.M., a plane flying dangerously low over Manhattan approached the World Trade Center and crashed into the upper floors of the North Tower (1 WTC). People in the street looked up and saw a huge explosion and fire that immediately broke out. They assumed that what they were witnessing was a tragic accident. Then at 9:03 A.M., another plane crashed into the South Tower (2 WTC). At that moment, it dawned on everyone watching the event either in person or on TV news that this could not be just a coincidence. Two planes would not crash into the World Trade Center at almost the same time. America was under attack.

The World Trade Center attack would cast a shadow over the decade.

The Pentagon's security was compromised in the attack.

The two planes had been hijacked in what turned out to be a well-coordinated plan. Five hijackers flew American Airlines Flight 11, en route from Boston to Los Angeles, into 1 WTC. Five other hijackers flew United Airlines Flight 175, also headed from Boston to Los Angeles, into 2 WTC.

Horrors continued to unfold throughout the day. At 9:37 A.M., five hijackers crashed American Airlines Flight 77 into the Pentagon just outside of Washington, D.C. The Pentagon sustained major damage. A fourth hijacked plane, United Airlines Flight 93, whose target was believed to be the White House or the Capitol building, crashed at 10:03 A.M. near Shanksville, Pennsylvania, when the passengers tried to take control of the plane from the four hijackers. Everyone on the plane died.

Fear quickly spread throughout the nation. There were rumored to be other hijacked planes still in the air. There were also bomb threats in various places. Meanwhile, back in lower Manhattan at 9:59 A.M., the South Tower of the World Trade Center totally collapsed in what resembled a controlled demolition. The building had been burning for only fifty-six minutes. Many people who worked in the floors below the point of impact of the plane had managed to escape in time. Terrified people ran through the streets to escape the burning debris and toxic clouds of smoke and dust from the collapsing tower.

At 10:28 A.M., the North Tower also collapsed after burning for 102 minutes. The surrounding buildings at the World Trade Center sustained varying amounts of damage. Later that day, at 5:21 P.M., 7 World Trade Center, a forty-seven-story office building, totally collapsed. Fires in the building caused by burning debris from the collapsing Twin Towers were probably responsible.

By the end of the day, about 3,000 people had died because of the attack. This included 340 firefighters and 60 police officers in New York. The World Trade Center site came to be known as Ground Zero.

The surrounding buildings were eventually repaired or rebuilt, and another impressive tall tower would replace the Twin Towers.

Why Do They Hate Us?

Americans wondered why the nineteen Islamic hijackers would willingly give up their own lives to carry out such a horrific terrorist attack on American soil. Why did they have such great hatred for us? Eight years earlier in February 1993, Islamic terrorists had set off a car bomb at the World Trade Center. On that day, they managed to kill six people and injure more than a thousand. This time they were determined to totally destroy the World Trade Center, and they succeeded.

The government immediately concluded that the 9/11 attack was the work of Osama bin Laden and al-Qaeda. Bin Laden had previously masterminded several bombings, including the American embassies in Kenya and Tanzania in 1998. In October 2000, al-Qaeda bombed the US warship USS *Cole* in Aden, Yemen.

President George Bush claimed that the terrorists hated us for our freedom and our American way of life. However, Osama bin Laden himself listed specific reasons for his hatred in his 2002 letter to America. Among these reasons were the presence of US military bases in the holy land of Saudi Arabia, US killing of Muslims in Somalia, the US sanctions against Iraq, and US support of Israel and various authoritarian regimes in the Middle East, such as Saudi Arabia, Egypt, and Jordan. He believed it was the duty of Muslims to wage a holy war against the United States.

The War on Terror

President Bush wanted to reassure the American people that their government would not rest until it had hunted down and gotten rid of all

Al-Qaeda leader Osama bin Laden was behind the 9/11 tragedy.

Soon after the attacks, President Bush declared a War on Terror.

the evildoers. On September 16, 2001, President Bush declared a war on terror. His message to the other nations of the world was, "Either you are with us, or you are with the terrorists." The Bush administration also recognized an Axis of Evil, consisting of Iraq, Iran, and North Korea. The list of targets in the coming war on terror started with Afghanistan, whose Taliban government was sheltering Osama bin Laden. The United States and its allies attacked Afghanistan on October 7, 2001. Next would come an invasion of Iraq in 2003.

Suspicious White Powder

Exactly one week after the 9/11 attacks, anonymous letters laced with mysterious white powder began appearing at media companies and congressional offices. The white powder turned out to be deadly anthrax spores. On October 4, Bob Stevens of American Media in Florida was hospitalized after he had inhaled anthrax. The next day, Stevens died. On October 12, an employee of NBC in New York tested positive for anthrax poisoning. Three days later, Senate Majority Leader Tom Daschle and Senator Patrick Leahy of Vermont reported that letters with anthrax were found in their offices.

In the following days, more cases of people suffering from anthrax poisoning were reported in Manhattan, New Jersey, and Washington D.C. On October 23, two postal workers in Washington were confirmed to have died from inhaling anthrax. On October 31, Kathy Nguyen, an employee of the Manhattan Eye, Ear, and Throat Hospital died from inhalation of anthrax. Then on November 21, Ottilie Lundgren in Connecticut became the fifth person to die from inhalation of anthrax.

People all around the country were afraid they had come across anthrax whenever they saw any kind of white powder. In one typical incident, commuters on a ferry that was about to take them across the bay from Sausalito to San Francisco were ordered to evacuate. Someone aboard the boat had reported finding white powder. After everyone had abandoned ship, it turned out that the suspicious white powder was sugar from a donut.

The FBI eventually accused Steven Hatfill, a government scientist, of sending the anthrax-laced letters. But he turned out to be innocent and sued the government. The FBI's next suspect, another government scientist named Bruce Ivins, commited suicide on July 29, 2008. He might have been the guilty party, but the evidence against him was inconclusive. So the identity of the anthrax perpetrator remained a mystery.

Protecting the Homeland

By now, the American people were so terrified that they would have gone along with just about any policies the government would have put into practice in the name of making the country safe. The anthrax attack was the last straw.

Government officials began referring to America as the homeland. Clearly there was now an urgent need to provide more security. So less than a month after the 9/11 attack, the Bush administration created the Department of Homeland Security (DHS). The purpose of this massive new bureaucracy was to prevent any acts of terrorism from occurring. In January 2002, a detention center was established at the Guantanamo Bay Naval Base in Cuba for dangerous prisoners in the war on terror.

The DHS came up with a color-coded terrorist warning system to let Americans know how frightened they should be at any particular time. Americans were told to be vigilant at all times and to report any suspicious behavior. "If you see something, say something," advised the DHS.

The DHS created the Transportation Security Administration (TSA) to provide security at airports. The hijacking of planes by the 9/11 terrorists showed that there was an obvious need to screen passengers boarding airplanes. Most Americans didn't object to the inconvenience of long lines going through security at the airport because it made them

Steven Hatfill maintained his innocence in sending the anthrax letters.

feel safer. They believed it was worth giving up a degree of privacy for greater security. First there was scanning of all carry-on baggage, which required compliance with a list of prohibited items. And there were routine electronic or physical body searches.

Then on December 22, 2001, al-Qaeda member Richard Reid was caught trying to detonate an explosive in his shoe aboard a flight from Paris to Miami. So of course, the TSA now required people to take their shoes off when going through security. Near the end of the decade, on Christmas Day 2009, Umar Farouk Abdulmutallab was caught trying to detonate plastic explosives in his underwear on a flight from Amsterdam to Detroit. In order to stop any future underwear bombers, the TSA eventually installed in many airports new full-body scanners that could see through a passenger's clothing and reveal everything hidden beneath.

In the next few years, there were terrorist bombings elsewhere in the world. Al-Qaeda carried out bombings in Bali, Jakarta, Casablanca, Mombassa, Riyadh, Istanbul, and other places. Other terrorists carried out bombings on commuter trains in Madrid in 2004 and in London on several underground lines and bus routes in July 2005. Many terrorist bombings also occurred in Moscow and other parts of Russia throughout the decade.

What Goes Up Must Come Down

The last three years of the 2000s were a difficult time for a great many Americans. Home prices, after shooting sharply higher for several years, began dropping in 2007. The housing collapse would continue until the end of the decade and beyond. The stock market also crashed, which added to America's ailing economy—that was already in serious trouble. Some of America's biggest corporations and financial institutions were about to go bankrupt or had already. Millions of people lost their jobs, in what came to be called the Great Recession.

The USA PATRIOT Act

The USA PATRIOT Act, an act of Congress, was signed into law by President Bush on October 26, 2001. The letters of USA PATRIOT actually stand for Uniting and Strengthening America by Providing Appropriate Tools Required to Intercept and Obstruct Terrorism. The act provided government agencies, for example the National Security Administration (NSA), greatly expanded powers of surveillance of individuals and groups suspected of terrorist-related activities. This included wiretaps, searches of business records, and searches of homes or offices without court orders, in effect making it much easier to spy on anyone in America. The government began eavesdropping on every citizen's phone calls and Internet activity including emails.

Most Americans were okey with the government's intrusion into their privacy, but some people were becoming concerned. They may have been reminded of words spoken by the great American patriot Benjamin Franklin in the eighteenth century, "They who can give up essential liberty to obtain a little temporary safety, deserve neither liberty nor safety." In the next decade, the NSA would come under a lot of criticism.

Millions more would lose their homes since those without jobs couldn't keep up with their monthly home mortgage payments. Many people had been encouraged by lenders to buy homes they could never really afford. Among these properties were large suburban homes known as McMansions. Now that home prices had dropped, many people owed more money on their home loans than the properties were worth. House flipping that had been so popular when house prices were rising continued on the way down. House flippers bought houses that were now in foreclosure and quickly sold them for a profit. Meanwhile, desperate unemployed people were willing to accept a job flipping burgers if they were lucky enough to get such a low-paying job.

No Place Like Home

During the 2000s, the cost of a college education had become more and more expensive. Many students had had to borrow money for their undergraduate college education. Upon graduating, they were faced with having to pay back loans of $25,000 or more. For many graduates, landing a job that paid enough to allow them to repay their student loans and also have enough money for living expenses was difficult. So after graduating, many young people moved back in with their parents in the homes they had grown up in. They became known as boomerang kids—leave home, go away to college, and then go back home.

By the end of the decade, a record number of young Americans, including those who had never gone to college, were living at home with their parents. In many towns and cities where housing prices had fallen, the cost of renting an apartment or house had remained high or even gone up. The high unemployment rate and high rents combined to persuade many young people to postpone marriage. In 2000, about 30 percent of 18- to 31-year-olds were in first marriages

The housing crisis caused many to lose their homes to foreclosure.

and living in their own homes. By 2009, only about 25 percent were married.

Social Media

Social media became a huge part of people's lives during the 2000s. Millions of Americans were spending increasing amounts of their time each day online sharing details of their personal life on various social networking websites. They generated content for the websites by posting status updates, photos—often selfies—and videos on every topic under the sun to an online audience consisting of friends, family members, and in many cases total strangers. For many, privacy seemed to become less important than it once was.

Friendster, founded in 2002, was the first general social network. It enabled people to meet new people online faster and more safely than in real life. You could easily expand your network of friends by including friends of friends. Many people actually used Friendster as a dating site.

LinkedIn, launched in 2003, became the world's largest business-oriented social networking service. It enabled people to post their resumes and apply for jobs online. It also allowed potential employers to find job applicants. LinkedIn served as a useful way for people to keep their professional lives online separate from their personal lives.

MySpace, founded in 2003, became the largest social networking site in the world by 2005. But in 2008 it was overtaken by Facebook, which had been created by Mark Zuckerberg in 2004. In 2009, Facebook had one hundred fifty million users, and each user had an average of more than one hundred Facebook friends. Zuckerberg claimed that his goal for Facebook was not to make money but to eventually connect every person in the world online. Indeed, by the middle of the next decade, Facebook would have more than one billion users.

Generation R

Many American victims of the Great Recession wondered how they would survive. Those who had not lost their jobs or homes worried that they might soon join those who had. Young people were very aware of the issues troubling their parents.

And they had their own reasons to worry. Would they be able to go to college? If already in college, would they be able to graduate? Would they ever find a job?

Even young children found things to worry about. *New York Times* reporter Steven Greenhouse sensed that a new generation had been born during the Great Recession. He coined the term Generation R—R for Recession—when writing about young Americans.

Facebook would become the most popular social media site.

Twitter, created in 2006, enabled users to send and read short 140-character messages called tweets. Registered users could read and post tweets, but unregistered users could only read them. Celebrities were the most popular tweeters on Twitter and many had thousands of followers.

Strange Shoes and Boots

Shoes with wheels implanted in the heels seems like a dangerous concept. Who would wear such shoes? Thousands of young kids zipping down the aisles of supermarkets, among other places, where they narrowly avoided colliding with shoppers. Apparently, many parents were happy to allow their kids to wear Heelys.

There was a time when if you noticed your shoes had a hole, you would visit the cobbler or else buy new shoes. But in 2006, it became quite fashionable to wear shoes with holes in them. Plastic shoes in wild bright colors with odd holes became popular. Some thought they were ugly, but the millions of people who loved their Crocs claimed they were very comfortable.

Then there were the popular shoes called Ugg boots. The Ugg boots were snuggly but ugly according to some. They were based on a type of boot that had been worn for many years by people herding sheep in Australia. According to an American podiatrist, Ugg Boots could be bad for the health of your feet because of the lack of arch and ankle support.

Wristbands: Serious and Silly

Yellow plastic wristbands with the word LIVESTRONG on them began appearing in May 2004. They were distributed by the Lance Armstrong Foundation to help raise awareness for cancer, and millions were sold. Teens, as well as adults, wore the yellow wristbands.

Catching Up With the News

By the end of the decade, nearly 80 percent of Americans were online, and about 60 percent of them used social networking sites. With each passing year, fewer Americans were reading newspapers for the latest news. Each year, more newspapers would go out of business. Instead of newspapers, people were relying on the Internet for news, especially on social media site updates. Facebook and Twitter made news a more participatory experience than before as people shared news articles and commented on other people's posts. Many writers, including journalists, posted blogs on their personal websites to present their views on current events in the news. To stay in business, major newspapers went online. The *New York Times*, which had gone online in 1996, went mobile in 2008 when it became available on the iPhone and iPod Touch.

Although some people were not aware of their purpose and just used them as a fashion statement, the Livestrong wristbands inspired other similar cause-related wristbands, such as pink wristbands for breast cancer awareness.

Silly Bandz were popular when they became available in 2008. The silicone rubber wristbands were invented by Rob Croak. The bright colored wristbands snapped back into the shape of various animals, fish, butterflies, unicorns, numbers, letters, and other things when taken off the wrist. Children loved them and collected and traded them.

The Mash-Up Decade

According to fashion experts, there was no one particular unique style of dress that jumped out as representing the 2000s. Rather, there were throwbacks to many different styles from past decades—mainly the 1960s, 1970s, 1980s, and 1990s—so it was appropriate to consider the hodge-podge of clothing styles in the 2000s a mash-up.

Women's fashion moved from a minimalist, unisex look early in the decade to more colorful, feminine, and dressy styles later on. Women wore denim miniskirts and jackets, tank-tops, flip-flops, and ripped jeans in the early years. Later they wore mostly low rise skinny jeans, tunics with wide or thin belts, longer tank-tops with a main blouse or shirt, leggings, knee-high boots with pointed toes, capri pants, and vintage clothing. In the late 2000s, women wore ballet flats, knitted sweater dresses, long shirts combined with a belt, leather jackets, and fur coats.

Men's fashion in the early 2000s had a cool, sporty look, featuring boot-cut jeans, light colored polo shirts, and baseball caps. Later on, men's styles were inspired by retro fashion from pop groups. These styles featured slim-fitting jeans, cartoon printed hoodies, Converse sneakers, mod-style parkas, and military dress jackets. In the late

2000s, men wore black leather jackets, Ed Hardy T-shirts, motorcycle boots, knitted V-neck sweaters, cardigans, and Ray Ban sunglasses. In men's business fashion, the classic suit with a three-buttoned jacket was replaced with a two-buttoned blazer worn with a matching suit trouser, a slim tie, and waistcoat.

By the end of the decade, men's fashion favored skinny jeans and beards.

Entertainment and the Arts

In the 2000s, huge numbers of Americans tuned into TV shows featuring the behavior of "real" people—or non-actors—in all sorts of challenging situations. But at the same time, wildly escapist movie fantasies also captured the imagination of millions who were eager for an break, however temporary, from the problems of the real world.

Reality TV

Reality TV is as old as the history of TV itself. Back in the 1940s, in the earliest days of broadcast TV, there were popular reality-type shows, such as Allen Funt's *Candid Camera* and *Queen for a Day*. Ted Mack's *Original Amateur Hour* and Arthur Godfrey's *Talent Scouts* featured amateur competition and audience voting. Game shows, such as *Beat the Clock* and *Truth or Consequences,* were big hits in the 1950s.

In 1973, a twelve-part PBS series *An American Family* showed a real family going through a divorce. Other popular reality TV of the 1960s and 1970s included competition shows, such as *The Dating Game* and The *Newlywed Game.* In the *The Gong Show,* participants were willing and in some cases eager to be humiliated for the chance to appear on live TV. In 1992, MTV debuted *The Real World*, in which seven strangers were picked to live together in a house and have their lives taped.

But in the 2000s, reality TV truly came into its own. TV producers realized that unscripted reality shows were much cheaper to produce than shows requiring scripts and a cast of actors. And they believed that there was a huge potential audience for new reality TV shows. The success of *Survivor* at the beginning of the decade showed that millions of Americans enjoyed watching real people struggling to survive in challenging situations. So a great variety of different types of reality shows debuted, and some of them were amazingly successful. Each popular reality show inspired the production of several others in a similar format.

Millions of Americans tuned in to the popular reality competition program *Survivor*, which has aired for more than thirty seasons.

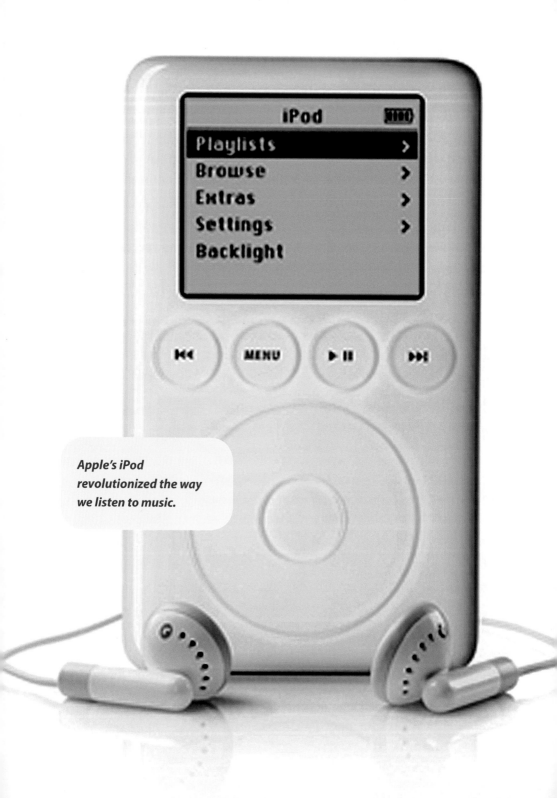

Apple's iPod revolutionized the way we listen to music.

Among the most successful reality TV shows that debuted in the United States in the 2000s were *Survivor* (2000), *The Amazing Race* (2001), *American Idol* (2002), *The Bachelor* (2002), *America's Next Top Model* (2003), *The Apprentice* (2004), *The Biggest Loser* (2004), *Dancing with the Stars* (2005), and *So You Think You Can Dance* (2005). Each of these shows was so successful that they lasted for many seasons and are still going strong today.

A Pocket Full of Music

Once upon a time, people placed a vinyl record on a phonograph turntable in order to listen to musical favorites from their record collection. With progress in the technology of recorded music, 78 rpm (revolutions per minute) records gave way to 45s and then 33s. Then came tape recorders and tape cassettes. This was followed by CDs (compact discs). Large collections of recorded music took up a lot of space in music lovers' homes. But early in the 2000s, a totally new way of collecting and experiencing music was born.

In October 2001, Americans had not yet gotten over the shock of the 9/11 attacks. Indeed, on October 23, people were afraid of being exposed to anthrax. Yet on that day, Steve Jobs, the CEO of Apple, walked onto the stage at Apple headquarters to make a historic announcement that would forever change the course of media and entertainment distribution. Jobs presented the first iPod, calling it a "breakthrough digital device." The small portable digital music player would actually let you carry one thousand songs in your pocket.

Back in January 2001, Apple had released iTunes, a software program that converted audio CDs into compressed digital audio files. In 2003 Apple launched the iTunes Music Store with two hundred thousand songs available for the iPod at 99 cents each. At the same time, Apple released its third generation iPod, which could hold seventy-five hundred songs. Sales of iPods were skyrocketing in America. In

June 2004, *Newsweek* magazine reported in a big cover story that America was an "iPod Nation." In October 2005, iTunes expanded to include TV shows and music videos. That month, Apple unveiled the new fifth generation iPod that played music and videos, as well as storing photos and games.

In December 2005, the White House revealed that President George Bush had an iPod. Among the artists he enjoyed listening to were the Beach Boys, the Beatles, and Aretha Franklin. In 2007 Apple released the iPhone. This Apple smartphone had essentially the same media capabilities as the iPod. In the next couple of years, it became just as popular as the iPod. By the middle of 2010, iPhone sales would overtake those of the iPod.

Meanwhile, the iPod was extremely popular throughout the 2000s. There were several different versions of the iPod—the iPod Mini, the iPod Shuffle, the iPod Nano, the iPod Classic, and the iPod Touch. And many Americans were happy carrying around their entire music collections in their pocket. On April 1, 2009, President Barack Obama gave an iPod to Queen Elizabeth II while on a visit to England. By the end of the decade, more than two hundred fifty million iPods had been sold, and the iTunes Store had sold almost ten billion songs.

Musical Fragmentation

There weren't any brand new musical styles or genres in the decade of the 2000s. All of the musical trends of the previous decades continued. Particular genres fragmented into sub-genres and sub-sub-genres. Just as in the world of fashion, mash-up could describe the world of music throughout the 2000s. What was different was the big change in the ways of listening to music. YouTube, iTunes, and peer-to-peer file sharing made it so easy to access any type of music or any group or artist. People who might have only been interested

Punk rock band Green Day released rock opera American Idiot *in 2004.*

Carrie Underwood dominated the country music charts.

in listening to one or a few particular artists or genres might now be willing to check out many different ones. Also, it was so easy to find whatever you were looking for.

Hip hop remained popular in the 2000s. The white rapper Eminem was the biggest hip hop act of the decade, as well as the best-selling overall music artist. Other hip hop stars of the 2000s included Kanye West, Jay-Z, Pharrell, Snoop Dogg, 50-Cent, Nelly, and many more. Pop rock stars included Kelly Clarkson, Alanis Morissette, and Demi Lovato. Clarkson was the winner of the first season of *American Idol* and became known as the Original American Idol. Canadian pop-punk singer Avril Lavigne sold more than thirty million albums. Nickelback, one of the biggest post-grunge bands of the 2000s, sold more than fifty million albums.

Other genres included nu metal, metalcore, hard rock and heavy metal, emo (songs that tended to be emotional or sad), garage rock, post punk, new wave revival, indie rock, and adult contemporary. Beyonce, Jennifer Lopez, Mary J. Blige, Usher, and Janet Jackson were among the biggest names in adult R&B. Justin Timberlake, Christina Aguilera, Britney Spears, Lady Gaga, Katy Perry, and Justin Bieber were big names in pop.

Country and electronic music were also popular throughout the 2000s. The biggest names in country included vocalists Carrie Underwood, an American Idol winner, and Taylor Swift. Vocalist Diana Krall was one of the decade's biggest names in jazz. And Grammy Award-winning singer-songwriter Norah Jones's music could best be described as a blending of mellow, acoustic pop with country, soul, and elements of jazz.

Death of a Giant

He was known as the King of Pop—Michael Jackson was a great singer, songwriter, record producer, dancer, and actor. Among his greatest hits were "Man in the Mirror," "Thriller," "Billie Jean," "Smooth Criminal," "Beat It," and "Earth Song." He died on June 25, 2009, at the age of fifty. He had health problems, and his death was caused by cardiac arrest. His death came as a shock to his millions of fans.

There was an outpouring of grief around the world. President Barack Obama sent a letter of condolence to the Jackson family. Nelson Mandela, the former president of South Africa, said that the loss of Jackson would be felt worldwide. Actress Elizabeth Taylor, Jackson's long-time friend, said she couldn't imagine life without him.

Jackson's funeral cost one million dollars. Howard Weitzman, a lawyer for Jackson's estate executors, said that a lavish funeral was appropriate because after all, "It was Michael Jackson. He was bigger than life when he was alive."

Amazing Worlds of Fantasy and Adventure

Perhaps because Americans had been so traumatized by the 9/11 attacks and the wars that followed, they would welcome any escape from the real world, however brief. Hollywood was only too happy to provide movies to transport them to other worlds. In these strange places, Americans watched with pleasure as heroes triumphed over evildoers.

Avatar

Possibly one of the most amazing movies of all time, *Avatar* was released in 2009. Director James Cameron's epic sci-fi hit transported audiences to the strange world Pandora in the year 2154, where the hero embarked on incredible adventures. When viewing Pandora's landscapes and its blue-skinned, ten-foot-tall inhabitants, the Na'vi, through 3-D glasses and on a giant IMAX screen, you could almost believe that you were there. The film made use of a new type of 3-D movie technology and a filming technique known as motion capture, where the recorded actions of human actors are used to animate digital character models.

The Big Screen

Among the most popular movies of the 2000s, which were based on books by J. R. R. Tolkien, was The Lord of the Rings trilogy: *The Fellowship of the Ring* (2001), *The Two Towers* (2002), and *The Return of the King* (2003). It also seemed that people could never get enough of the young hero Harry Potter, and new sequels about the young hero kept coming throughout the decade: *Harry Potter and the Sorcerer's Stone* (2001), *Harry Potter and the Chamber of Secrets* (2002), *Harry Potter and the Prisoner of Azkaban* (2004), *Harry Potter and the Goblet of Fire* (2005), and *Harry Potter and the Order of the Phoenix* (2007).

Also popular was a wonderful fantasy adapted from a book by C. S. Lewis called *The Chronicles of Narnia: The Lion, the Witch, and the Wardrobe* (2005). Americans also loved movies about superheroes, especially *Batman* and *Spiderman*. There were also two new *Star Wars* movies: *Star Wars: Episode II: Attack of the Clones* (2002) and *Star Wars: Episode III: Revenge of the Sith* (2005). And a new *Star Trek* film was released in 2009.

The Lord of the Rings *trilogy was an eight-year undertaking.*

NASCAR racer Dale Earnhardt was killed during a collision.

Sports

The 2000s may have been a difficult decade for many Americans, but that didn't spoil their enjoyment of their favorite sports. There were many thrilling moments in NASCAR races and team sport events, as well as in Olympic competitions. As always, many records would be broken by amazing athletes whose dreams, hard work, and dedication to their sport made it happen.

Thrills at Every Turn

Professional auto racing is an exciting sport. It is also very popular, as shown by the crowds of fans at NASCAR (National Association for Stock Car Auto Racing) events, the Indianapolis 500, and other races. The biggest events draw crowds of up to two hundred fifty thousand to three hundred thousand spectators. However, car racing is also dangerous. Drivers go as fast as two hundred miles per hour—sometimes more. Car crashes occur frequently, and drivers are often seriously injured and sometimes even killed.

Dale Earnhardt had become famous by driving stock cars for NASCAR. His track record included seven Winston Cup championships, and he was winner of the Daytona 500 at the Daytona International Speedway in 1998. The Daytona 500 is a NASCAR event, and the 500 refers to the five hundred miles the drivers have to complete.

On February 18, 2001, Earnhardt was in Daytona Beach, Florida, racing again in the Daytona 500. Like so many other races, this one had been exciting. As the drivers were into the last lap, tragedy struck. At Turn 4, Earnhardt lost traction inside the track. This caused his car to make a sharp right turn toward the outside wall. At this moment, a car driven by Ken Schrader was between Earnhardt and the wall. Earnhardt slammed into Schrader's car. Unfortunately, there had been no way that Schrader could have avoided the crash. Schrader walked away from the crash, but Dale Earnhardt was killed instantly.

Earnhardt was the fourth driver to die in NASCAR races within a year. As a result of these tragedies, the NASCAR organization mandated head-and-neck restraints and several other safety features for racing cars.

Going for the Gold in Beijing

"Records are always made to be broken no matter what they are. Anybody can do anything that they set their mind to," said American swimmer Michael Phelps after winning his eighth gold medal in the 2008 summer Olympics in Beijing.

Phelps had started swimming at the age of seven. By the time he was fifteen, he qualified for the US Olympic swim team, and he swam in the 2000 Summer Olympics in Sydney, Australia. The following year he broke the world record in the 200-meter butterfly to become the youngest man ever to set a swimming world record.

Phelps went on to win many medals in each of the following years, including four gold medals in the 2004 Summer Olympics in Long Beach, California. In Beijing in 2008, he would win eight gold medals and set new world records. In the 400-meter individual medley, he broke his previous world record by nearly two seconds and won

Michael Phelps became the most decorated Olympian of all time.

Born to Race

Danica Patrick is another American who gained fame in the world of professional auto racing. She also works as a model and an advertising spokeswoman. But most of all, she loves auto racing, which had captured her imagination when she was a young girl. At the age of ten, she began go-karting at the Sugar River Raceway in Brodhead, Wisconsin. She moved to England at the age of sixteen to participate in various racing events.

In the United States in the 2000s, Patrick raced in many professional events and gained indispensable experience. In 2005 she became the fourth woman to compete in the Indy 500. Patrick was named Rookie of the Year for her outstanding driving in the 2005 Indianapolis 500 and the 2005 Indy Car Series season. In 2008, Patrick won her first Indy Racing League (IRL) race at the 2008 Indy Japan 300 and became the first woman to win an Indy Car Series race.

the first of eight gold medals. He finished the first leg of the 4x100-meter freestyle in 47.51 seconds and won his second gold medal. He set another world record by completing the 4x100-meter freestyle in 3:08:24.

Next came the 200-meter freestyle, in which Phelps won his third gold medal. He finished in 1:42:96, which broke his previous world record and set his third world record at the Olympics. Phelps got his fourth gold medal the next day in the 200-meter butterfly. He set another world record by finishing in 1:52:03. Less than one hour later he won his fifth gold medal and set his fifth world record when he swam the lead-off leg of the 4x200-meter freestyle relay, which the American team finished in 6:58:56.

Two days later, Phelps was at it again. He won his sixth gold medal by finishing the 200-meter individual medley in 1:54:23, which also set his sixth world record. Next day, he won his seventh gold by finishing the 100-meter butterfly in 50:58. By this time, Phelps began to feel like he was in a dream world where anything was possible. He said that he had to pinch himself to make sure he wasn't dreaming.

The next day, August 17, Phelps won his eighth gold medal in the 4x100-meter medley relay. Phelps and his three teammates set a new world record of 3:29:34. He had broken the record of seven gold medals won in a single Olympic Games by Mark Spitz in 1972.

Making Baseball History

He is the son of former San Francisco Giant right fielder Bobby Bonds and the godson of Willie Mays. Growing up under the influence of such baseball greats, it is not surprising that Barry Bonds would also someday make a name for himself in Major League baseball.

Barry Bonds played as a left fielder for the Pittsburgh Pirates from 1986 to 1992 and for the San Francisco Giants from 1993 to 2007. Along the way, he won seven Most Valuable Player (MVP) awards—

Fastest Man on Earth

Another amazing athlete going for the gold in the Beijing Olympics was Usain Bolt, a sprinter from Jamaica. At age fifteen, he was already impressing the world with his lightning speed and had won the 200-meter dash at the 2002 World Junior Championships in Kingston, Jamaica. This made him the youngest World Junior gold medalist ever.

In Beijing, Bolt won the 100-meter sprint in a record-setting 9.69 seconds. He then won the 200-meter sprint in 19.30 seconds, which set another record. Bolt won two gold medals for these sprints. He then won a third gold medal two days later as the third leg in the Jamaican 4x100 meters relay team. Usain Bolt would continue to break sprint records in the coming years. He is regarded as the fastest person in the world.

the most for any player—and eight Golden Glove Awards. On August 7, 2007, Bonds broke Hank Aaron's all-time Major League baseball record of 755 home runs. Sadly, the Giants did not renew Bonds' contract for the 2008 season. The new home run king's Major League career had come to an end.

So what happened? Apparently, Bonds had become involved in a scandal involving the use of steroids—performance enhancing drugs—by baseball players. And Barry Bonds, possibly the greatest baseball player of all time, has not been inducted into the Baseball Hall of Fame because of his suspected use of steroids.

Mr. Basketball

LeBron James was given a basketball and hoop as a Christmas present in 1988 just a few days before his fourth birthday. He went wild with joy and immediately ran up to the hoop and slam-dunked the ball. One of the world's greatest basketball players had just been born.

By 2001, James had become a champ and led his high school team to one victory after another. That year he was named Ohio's Mr. Basketball. The next year, 2002, James appeared on the cover of *Sports Illustrated*. After graduating in 2003, James was selected to play on the Cleveland Cavaliers of the National Basketball Association (NBA). His fame grew as basketball fans across the nation watched James play on TV. He quickly became a basketball superstar.

James was named Rookie of the Year in the 2003-2004 basketball season. He would continue to win one award after another throughout the rest of the decade. In the 2008 summer Olympics in Beijing, James helped Team USA win its first gold medal since 2000. He won the NBA Most Valuable Player (MVP) award in the 2008-2009 basketball season and again in the 2009-2010 season.

National and International Politics

The two presidential elections during the 2000s were unusual. In 2000, the race between Al Gore and George Bush was so close that the US Supreme Court decided the outcome and handed the presidency to Bush. In 2008, America elected its first African American president. Tired of endless war in Iraq and Afghanistan and frightened by a collapsing economy, voters chose Barack Obama. They hoped he would bring about the changes he promised.

A Close Election

This was one of the closest electoral contests in the history of the United States. In the 2000 presidential election—between the Democrat candidate, Vice President Al Gore, and the Republican governor of Texas, George W. Bush—the final outcome depended on how the vote went in Florida. Weeks after Election Day, supporters of Gore and Bush were still arguing about who won the election. To win, either candidate needed two hundred seventy electoral votes. In Florida, Bush and Gore had each received about 49 percent of the vote. And both candidates needed Florida's twenty-five electoral votes to win.

Vice President Al Gore ran against George W. Bush for the presidency.

Pakistani Muslims had joined the mujahideen to fight the Soviets.

After weeks of court battles and disagreements during vote recounts—mostly about how to interpret any ballots that had been improperly punched—the Florida Supreme Court ordered certain counties to recount their ballots. The Bush group protested that decision, and the case went to the US Supreme Court. A five-to-four conservative majority on the US Supreme Court ruled that a complete recount in Florida would be unconstitutional because different counties had different ways of counting the votes.

At that point, Al Gore was behind by only a few hundred votes in Florida and had been gaining ground with each attempt at a recount. By preventing a complete tally, the Supreme Court justices handed Florida's twenty-five electoral votes and the presidency to George Bush. The electoral vote was now 271 for Bush, 266 for Gore. Al Gore, who was actually more than a half million votes ahead of Bush in the nation's popular vote, conceded the election to Bush. Many Democratic voters in America were angry and believed that the election had been stolen. On January 20, 2001, George W. Bush was inaugurated as the 43rd president of the United States.

America Invades Afghanistan

Back in the 1980s during the Soviet Union's occupation of Afghanistan, the United States helped organize, arm, and train an Islamic resistance to the Soviets. Known as *mujahideen*, these radical Islamic fighters consisted of Afghans, as well as fighters from Pakistan and various Middle Eastern countries who came to Afghanistan to join the anti-Soviet jihad. Among the *mujahideen* was a wealthy Saudi by the name of Osama bin Laden. In 1989, when the Soviets were eventually defeated and had withdrawn from Afghanistan, bin Laden turned against his former supporter, the United States. He then began organizing his group of terrorists known as al-Qaeda.

Years of warfare in Afghanistan between rival Islamic groups followed the withdrawal of the Soviets. By 1996, the Taliban, who were ethnic Pashtun tribesmen under the leadership of Mullah Omar, controlled most of the country. Opposed to the Taliban was the Northern Alliance, which was composed of ethnic minority Tajiks, Uzbeks, and Hazaras. The Taliban provided sanctuary for bin Laden and al-Qaeda and gave them a base from which they could plan and carry out attacks in other countries.

On September 9, 2001, al-Qaeda assassinated Ahmad Shah Massoud, the Tajik commander of the Northern Alliance. This assured Taliban protection for bin Laden after the attacks on the United States two days later. In a speech to the American people on September 20, nine days after the attacks, Bush demanded that the Taliban immediately hand over the al-Qaeda leaders hiding in their land or they would share in their fate.

By October 7, 2001, it had become clear that the Taliban were not willing to comply with Bush's demands. So on that day, the United States with British support, launched Operation Enduring Freedom and began air strikes on Taliban and al-Qaeda forces in Afghanistan. Soon after, American ground forces arrived and began joint operations with the Northern Alliance.

By early December, the Taliban had been mostly defeated. Taliban leaders had escaped across the border to find refuge in the northern border regions of Pakistan. Meanwhile, bin Laden and his al-Qaeda fighters, along with some Taliban members, had taken shelter in a system of caves in the Tora Bora Mountains close to the Pakistan border. They were attacked there by US and Northern Alliance forces. But when the battle was over, bin Laden was nowhere to be seen. Apparently, he had managed to escape across the border into Pakistan.

The United States had overthrown the Taliban, and the first part of the War in Afghanistan was over. But American troops would remain

An Afghan man holds a portrait of Ahmad Shah Massoud.

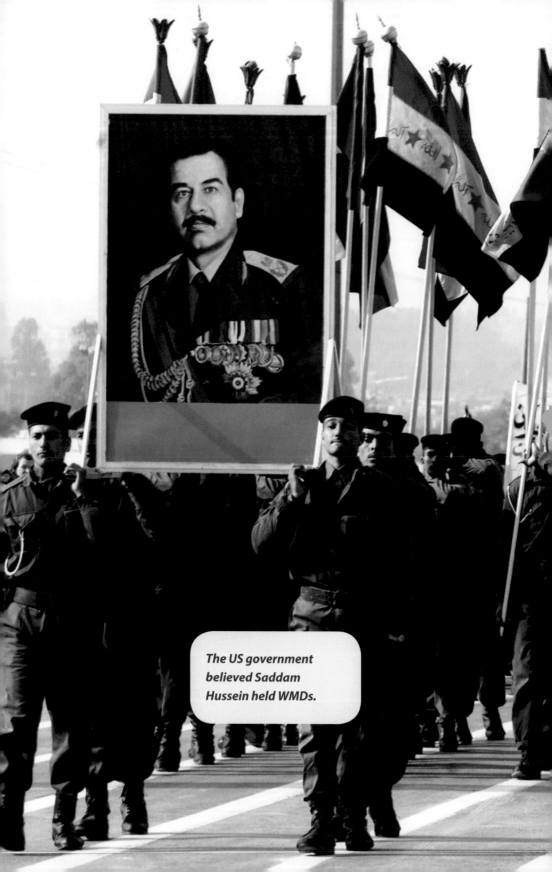

The US government believed Saddam Hussein held WMDs.

in Afghanistan for the rest of the decade and beyond, engaged in what would become America's longest war. The Bush administration would embark on the difficult job of nation building. Among the most important tasks would be creating a government and restoring the rights of Afghan women. Under the Taliban, women had no rights and were required to wear the all-covering burqa. An Afghan government was established under the leadership of Hamid Karzai. Fighting against the Taliban would continue on and off in different parts of the country.

Meanwhile, after Tora Bora, the American's pursuit of Osama bin Laden had taken a back seat to a new military goal. The Bush administration had now set its sights on Saddam Hussein, the dictator of Iraq.

Weapons of Mass Destruction?

Iraq's dictator Saddam Hussein was allowed to remain in power after his defeat in the Persian Gulf War in 1991 by the UN Coalition. At the time, many thought that this was a mistake. After the signing of the cease-fire agreement, the United Nations required Saddam Hussein to agree to eliminate his weapons of mass destruction and allow UN weapons inspectors to monitor the agreement. The UN Security Council also imposed economic sanctions on Iraq, causing tremendous hardship for the Iraqi people.

Relations between the United States and Iraq remained tense throughout the 1990s. On June 26, 1993, President Bill Clinton ordered a missile attack on the Iraqi Intelligence Service (ISS) command center in Baghdad for its attempted assassination of former President George H. W. Bush. In 1996, Clinton ordered waves of missiles against Iraqi air defense targets in response to Saddam Hussein's attempt to launch an attack against Iraqi Kurdistan.

In his 1998 State of the Union Address, Clinton, after mentioning the successful work of the UN weapons inspectors, warned Congress of Saddam Hussein's possible continual pursuit of nuclear weapons.

Later that year, on October 31, Clinton signed the Iraq Liberation Act into law, which called for a regime change in Iraq. In December 1998, Clinton ordered air strikes against military instillations in Iraq when Saddam Hussein refused to fully cooperate with UN weapons inspectors. After the bombing, Saddam Hussein blocked any further UN inspections.

During the presidential election campaign in 2000, the Republican Party platform called for full implementation of the Iraq Liberation Act. In other words, Saddam Hussein must be removed from power. Right after the 9/11 attacks, the George Bush administration began planning an invasion of Iraq. Administration officials began dropping hints of a secret relationship between Saddam Hussein and al-Qaeda. And there was a lot more talk of Saddam's weapons of mass destruction.

On November 13, 2002, weapons inspectors returned to Iraq. But by February 2003, they had found no new evidence of any significant amount of prohibited items. On February 13, 2003, Secretary of State Colin Powell went to the United Nations seeking to gain authorization for the invasion of Iraq. In his address to the UN General Assembly, he presented evidence of a mobile biological weapons lab, which his source later admitted to be fraudulent.

The United Nations did not grant authorization to proceed with the invasion. Nevertheless, plans went ahead. Most Americans supported an invasion of Iraq. But many protests by antiwar demonstrators took place in the United States and abroad. Indeed, on February 15, 2003, at least six million and possibly as many as ten million people took part in worldwide protests against a war in Iraq.

In his March 17, 2003, address to the nation, President Bush demanded that Saddam Hussein and his two sons surrender and leave Iraq. He gave them forty-eight hours. But the next day, on March 18,

Coalition of the Willing

In his September 12, 2002 Address to the UN Security Council, George Bush made the case for an invasion of Iraq. But some key members, such as France and Russia, favored diplomacy rather than war. The Bush administration then put together a coalition of nations willing to join the United States in the invasion.

This Coalition of the Willing included forty-nine nations, although only seven were willing to provide troops—the United States, United Kingdom, Australia, Poland, Spain, Italy, and Denmark. On October 16, in a vote in the US Congress, the Authorization for the Use of Military Force Against Iraq Resolution of 2002 was passed by 70 percent of the House and Senate.

the United States began bombing Iraq. As in Afghanistan, a war that was easy to start would be difficult to end.

And what about those weapons of mass destruction—the main stated reason for invading Iraq? They were never found.

Mistakes Were Made

President Bush announced the start of the Iraq War on March 20, 2003. The war in Iraq would drag on until the end of the decade and beyond. Administration war planners had predicted the war would be over quickly. The grateful Iraqi people would shower US troops with flowers for ridding them of their brutal dictator, Saddam Hussein. In the early going, an easy victory seemed a sure thing. The bombing of Baghdad, which the United States called Shock and Awe, sent senior Iraqi leaders into hiding. The Iraqi residents of the city paid with the destruction of lives and infrastructure.

The Iraqi army fled before US ground forces moving north toward Baghdad. On April 9th, Baghdad came under US control. Joyful residents toppled statues of Saddam Hussein. There was wide-scale looting of government offices. Less than one month later, on May 1, Bush landed on the aircraft carrier *Abraham Lincoln* and announced an early victory in the war against Saddam Hussein. Above Bush was a banner that read "Mission Accomplished."

The invasion of Iraq now transitioned into the next phase—the occupation of Iraq. This would prove to be much more difficult, and there would not be anymore "Mission Accomplished" declarations for a long, long time, if ever.

One mistake by the American administrators of the occupation was the disbanding of the Iraqi army, which sent hundreds of thousands of armed Iraqi men into unemployment and desperation. Iraq would descend into years of chaos. There were suicide bombings, kidnappings, warfare between different sects of Islam—Sunni vs. Shia—creation of radical Islamic terror groups allied with al-Qaeda, the deaths of hundreds of thousands of Iraqi men, women, and children, untold numbers of injured, millions of displaced persons, and general widespread devastation. Coalition forces also suffered high casualties, mostly from improvised explosive devices, or IEDs.

And what of Saddam Hussein? On December 9, 2003, the Iraqi dictator, who had been in hiding for nine months, was discovered by US soldiers crouching in an eight-foot hole at a farm outside Tikrit, his hometown. He was arrested without a fight. After spending the next three years in prison and having two trials, Saddam Hussein would be executed in December 2006.

Some aspects of American treatment of Iraqis inspired hatred for the United States throughout the Islamic world. In April 2004, news spread of the torture and humiliation of Iraqi prisoners by their American guards in the Abu Ghraib prison west of Baghdad. There were many other reported instances of abusive treatment of Iraqis elsewhere. Later, whenever asked why some things had gone so wrong in Iraq, senior American officials would often just say, "mistakes were made."

But there was some good news. American attempts at nation building led to an Iraqi presidential election on January 30, 2005. Huge numbers of Iraqi men and women voted in the country's first free election in fifty years. There was great enthusiasm among the people in spite of death threats and suicide bombings. On December 15, 2005, millions of Iraqis elected a Parliament to a four-year term. In April 2006, Nuri al-Maliki became the leader of Iraq's first full-term government since the fall of Saddam Hussein.

On November 17, 2008, the Iraqi Parliament ratified a status of forces agreement with the United States, which laid out a plan for ending America's military role in the war. American troops would be required to pull out of most Iraqi cities by the summer of 2009. The last

The Great Divide

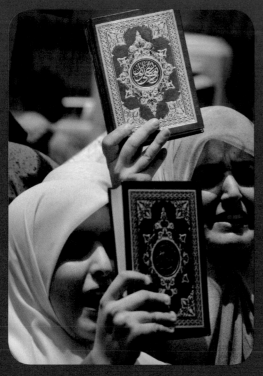

Soon after the death of the prophet Muhammad in the year 632, Muslims split into two sects—Sunni and Shia. There was a dispute over who should be the leader, or caliph, of the Islamic world. The Sunni, the majority of Muslims at about 90 percent, believe that Abu Bakr, the father of Muhammad's wife Aisha, was Muhammad's rightful successor. The Shias believe that Muhammad ordained his cousin and son-in-law Ali Ibn Abi Talib and his direct descendants to be his successors. Down through the centuries, there have been periods of cooperation between the two Islamic sects, and there have been times of conflict. All Muslims consider the Quran to be divine. But the two sects differ in their interpretation of hadith, the reported teachings, deeds, and sayings of the prophet Muhammad.

American combat troops would have to leave Iraq by the end of 2011. The war would end not with a final battle, but with a final march home.

Yes We Can

By 2008, the American people were ready for a change. Many were struggling to survive the effects of the crash in the housing and financial markets. They were tired of the nation's wars in Iraq and Afghanistan, where there did not seem to be any light at the end of the tunnel. They were tired of President George Bush, who in nearing the end of his second term had worn out his welcome. His popularity rating in the polls had sunk to a new low. By now, many Americans believed that the nation should never have gone to war against Iraq. After all, fifteen of the nineteen 9/11 hijackers had been Saudis, not Iraqis. And people remembered the poor job done by the Bush administration in helping New Orleans recover from the devastation of Hurricane Katrina in 2005. In addition, people blamed the government for allowing the nation to slide into such a frightening recession.

In the 2008 presidential campaign season, the time seemed ripe for a candidate who could convince America that he or she could bring about the changes so many longed for. Barack Obama, with his multiracial heritage, was certainly different from the usual candidates. His father, Barck Obama Sr., was from Kenya, and his mother, Ann Dunham, was of English ancestry. Barack Obama was born in Hawaii in 1961. After his parents were divorced, Ann married Lolo Soetoro, a student from Indonesia. The family moved to Indonesia, where Barack attended school from the ages of six to ten. Then, Ann and Lolo separated, and Ann took Barack back to Hawaii. Obama has spoken of how his worldview was formed by his experiences of a variety of cultures while growing up.

After Barack Obama graduated from Harvard Law School in 1991, he moved to Chicago. There he worked as a lawyer in civil rights legislation and neighborhood economic development. He then taught Constitutional law at the University of Chicago. He was elected to the Illinois State Senate in 1996 and served as State Senator from 1997 to 2004.

On October 2, 2002, President Bush and Congress agreed on the joint resolution authorizing the Iraq War. On that day, Obama spoke out against the war at an anti-Iraq War rally in Chicago. He

Barack Obama became the first African-American president.

would become known for his rousing speeches. On July 27, 2004, Obama delivered the keynote address at the 2004 Democratic National Convention. It was this speech, seen on TV by more than nine million viewers, that put Obama on the map. In November 2004, Obama was elected as a US Senator from Illinois.

Obama was still serving in the US Senate in 2008 while campaigning for the presidency. Obama and his organization ran a brilliant campaign that made good use of the Internet to reach out to people. On June 3, after the last of the primaries had taken place, Obama announced that he had secured the majority of the delegates necessary to win the democratic nomination for President. On June 7th, Senator Hillary Clinton conceded the race to Obama. On August 23, Obama chose Senator Joe Biden to be his running mate.

In his campaign speeches, Obama inspired people with the slogans "Change We Can Believe In" and "Yes We Can." He truly did appear to be different and did seem to represent change. He told Americans what they wanted to hear. Whatever change you wished for, you could imagine that that was the change Obama was promising.

On November 4, 2008, Obama won the presidential election. He easily defeated his Republican opponent John McCain by receiving 52.9 percent of the popular vote and 365 electoral votes compared to McCain's 45.6 percent of the popular vote and 173 electoral votes. America had elected the nation's first African American president. On January 20, 2009, an exciting day in America, Barack Obama was inaugurated as the 44th president of the United States.

The Recovery Begins

As soon as President Obama took office in January 2009, his first priority was to prevent the Great Recession from becoming another

Great Depression. America's economy was collapsing, and the nation was losing about eight hundred thousand jobs a month. Obama and his economic advisors created legislation called the American Recovery and Reinvestment Act of 2009 (ARRA). Also called the Stimulus, the act provided $787 billion dollars to be spent on tax cuts and credits, propping up state budgets, and for infrastructure and investment.

Republicans refused to cooperate with President Obama's efforts to save the nation. On January 26th, the bill passed by a 244 to 188 vote in the House of Representatives. All but eleven Democrats voted for the bill. All Republicans voted against it except one who didn't vote. On February 7, the bill passed in the Senate by a vote of 61 to 37, with one not voting. All Democrats voted in favor of the bill, but only three Republicans voted for it. On February 17, Obama signed the Recovery Act into law.

Obama then began working on the Affordable Care Act (ACA) to make health care more affordable. Here, too, he was faced with fierce Republican opposition. But on March 23, 2010, Obama signed the ACA, which would become known as ObamaCare, into law.

No You Can't

As Obama was being inaugurated, a group of key Republicans were holding a meeting. They agreed that their main goal over the next four years would be to ruin the presidency of Barack Obama. Indeed, they would fulfill their roles as spoilers as best they could. Obama was well aware of the differences in political beliefs and priorities between Democrats and Republicans. He believed that the most effective way to accomplish his goals would be to try to bridge the divide to reach out to Republicans in a spirit of realistic compromise. However, the typical Republican response to any Obama initiative was an automatic "NO," as if that represented a serious policy.

Advances in Science, Technology, and Medicine

During the 2000s, tourists ventured into space for the first time. Of course, these trips were not for everyone. The first space tourist had to pay twenty million dollars for a seat on a Russian Soyuz spacecraft. Meanwhile back on earth, people were dealing with catastrophic earthquakes and tsunamis, as well as extreme weather events, which scientists blamed on global warming.

To Boldly Go Where No Tourist Had Gone Before

Sixty-one year old Dennis Tito, an American businessman, had made a fortune in the world of finance. Earlier in his life, he had worked as an engineer at NASA's Jet Propulsion Laboratory. But throughout all these years, he never forgot his dream. It was now forty years since Yuri Gagarin, the Russian cosmonaut, had become the first person in space. At the time, Tito was so excited he could think of nothing else. He made up his mind that someday he, too, would fly in space.

In 2001, Dennis Tito became the world's first space tourist. Space Adventures, a Virginia company, arranged for Tito's eight-day space mission with Russia's Federal Space Agency. Tito paid $20 million to make his lifelong dream a reality. Before heading for space, Tito had

Former NASA engineer Dennis Tito became the world's first space tourist.

Apple CEO Steve Jobs announced the first iPhone in 2007.

to spend eight months in Russia training at Star City outside of Moscow. NASA and the space agencies of several other partners in the orbiting International Space Station (ISS) recommended against Tito's mission. They were afraid he might get in the way of busy astronauts working on the station. And they were concerned that at his age, Tito might have health issues in space that could pose problems for the crew.

But on April 28, 2001, Tito blasted off for the International Space Station with Russian cosmonauts aboard a Russian Soyuz spacecraft. Tito's space mission turned out to be a total success. In the years that followed, several more tourists ventured into space.

On February 1, 2003, the *Columbia* space shuttle disaster was a reminder that space travel could still be very dangerous. As it was reentering earth's atmosphere, *Columbia* disintegrated over Texas and Louisiana. All seven crew members were killed. But this tragedy did not stop brave tourists from traveling into space. In 2006, the fourth space tourist, Dallas businesswoman Anousheh Ansari, became the first female space tourist.

Going Mobile

In the 2000s, new developments in computer technology would bring about major changes in the way people communicated. Cell phones had become very popular in the 1990s, especially flip phones. But a new type of cell phone, known as a smartphone, became most people's choice in the 2000s. In 2007, Apple introduced its first iPhone. At the time, business reporters were skeptical that anything would come of it. According to a report in Bloomberg Finance, "The iPhone is nothing more than a luxury bauble that will appeal to a few gadget freaks. In terms of its impact on the industry, the iPhone is less relevant."

The iPhone then went on to become the most popular cell phone. Americans were happy to get rid of their dumb phone and begin using a smartphone. The new phones were amazingly sophisticated mobile

The Space Shuttle *Columbia* Disaster

On January 23, 2003, the Space Shuttle *Columbia* blasted off from the Kennedy Space Center in Florida on its twenty-eigth mission. For sixteen days *Columbia* orbited the earth while the crew conducted science experiments. The seven-member crew consisted of Rick D. Husband, William C. McCool, David M. Brown, Kalpana Chawla, Michael P. Anderson, Laurel B. Clark, and Ilan Ramon. Eighty-two seconds after *Columbia's* launch, a piece of foam insulation about the size of a suitcase broke off from the external fuel tank. The foam chunk struck the left wing and created a six- to ten-inch hole in it. This would allow hot gases to enter the wing when *Columbia* reentered the atmosphere before landing.

On February 1, *Columbia* reentered the atmosphere at four hundred thousand feet above the Pacific Ocean. About fifteen minutes later, *Columbia* broke apart over Texas and killed the crew. In the decade that saw the first tourists heading into space, the fate of the Space Shuttle *Columbia* showed that space travel could still be extremely dangerous.

computers. In addition to making phone calls, you could go online, text or send emails, read maps, take and send pictures and videos, and play games. Many people began using their new mobile computers instead of their desktop or laptop computers.

Many Americans were also using another new mobile electronic device called the Kindle. Introduced in 2007 by Amazon, the Kindle was designed for reading eBooks. It proved to be a very convenient product. You could take it anywhere, and it was easier than carrying books around.

PackBots to the Rescue

In the days right after the collapse of the World Trade Center buildings on 9/11, there was a frantic search going on at Ground Zero for any possible survivors buried in the rubble. This was very difficult and dangerous work, as huge fires were still burning and sections of the rubble were unstable.

A professor of computer science and robotics named Robin Murphy decided that this was a job for PackBots. The PackBots, made by the iRobot company, were about the size of a shoebox. They had tank-like treads on their wheels and shipping-crane arms. Murphy brought two PackBots to Ground Zero and put them to work.

The PackBots were able to get into small spaces that no human could have. They could also withstand the intense heat from the fires. So the PackBots searched through the rubble and sent back images from hard-to-reach spaces. Unfortunately, the PackBots did not find any survivors. But they came in handy for assessing the structural integrity of the debris and damaged buildings that were still standing. This was the first use of PackBots in a disaster, but it would not be the last such use of a robot.

Small flying robots were used in New Orleans when much of the city was underwater after being struck by Hurricane Katrina in 2005.

The robots flew over flooded areas and looked for survivors. In the future, more sophisticated robots would prove useful in disasters, both natural and manmade.

Coming of the Cyborgs

In the 1970s, a sci-fi book by Martin Caidin called *Cyborg* became a bestseller. The popular book was then partially used for a TV series, *The Six Million Dollar Man*, about a bionic man. In the TV series, which ran from 1973 to 1978, former astronaut Steve Austin, played by Lee Majors, is horribly injured in the crash of an experimental plane. Doctors save his life with bionic replacements for various parts of his body. Austin has been transformed into a cyborg—a man that is part human, part machine.

Jumping ahead to the 2000s, science fiction began to merge with reality. In 2001, Jesse Sullivan became the world's first bionic man. In May of that year, fifty-four-year-old Sullivan was so severely injured while working as a high-power electrical lineman that both arms had to be amputated. The Rehabilitation Institute of Chicago (RIC) replaced his arms with experimental bionic, or thought-controlled, prosthetic arms. Sullivan's bionic arms were activated by his own thought-generated nerve impulses. Sullivan was now able to do routine tasks, such as putting on socks, taking out the garbage, carrying groceries, and vacuuming.

Then in 2009, an Italian named Pierpaolo Petruziello lost his left forearm in a car crash. A four-fingered hand, called LifeHand, was linked to the stump of his arm by electrodes. Petruziello could control complex movements of the hand and fingers using only his mind. In the future, scientific progress will lead to a world in which true cyborgs will walk among us.

US Army Ranger Bill Dunham walks with a smart prosthesis.

The HPV vaccine Gardasil was developed to prevent cervical cancer.

New Vaccines Against HPV

The most common sexually transmitted disease (STD) in the United States is called human papillomavirus (HPV). There are more than a hundred types of this virus, and most people have at least one type. It is estimated that 75 to 80 percent of sexually active adults have or have had HPV. In most cases, HPV never goes away once you have become infected. Many people infected by HPV develop genital warts. For some people, HPV can be dangerous.

Each year, hundreds of thousands of women and girls in the United States develop infections from HPV. Among this group, more than ten thousand develop cervical cancer and thirty-seven hundred die from the cancer. Scientists knew that cervical cancer is unique among cancers caused by infection because every case of cervical cancer is associated with an HPV infection. This being the case, a vaccine against HPV would be an effective way of preventing cervical cancer. This led to the development of Gardasil.

The Food and Drug Administration, or FDA, first approved the use of Gardasil for females and males, ages nine to twenty-six, on June 8, 2006. In 2009, the FDA approved another HPV vaccine called Cervarix. It was only approved for females, though, from the age of ten through twenty-five. Cervarix only provides protection against HPV strains 16 and 18.

Three Years, Three Nightmares

Amazing as it seems, it was the hottest summer in Europe since the year 1540. The summer of 2003 brought absolute misery to millions of people throughout Europe. The intense heat wave in August killed more than seventy thousand people. France was hit the worst with

14,802 heat-related deaths. People in many parts of Europe did not know how to cope with the heat. After all, summers were typically pleasant, especially in France. So most people did not have air conditioners. People did not realize they had to make sure to keep hydrated. Most of the people who died were elderly persons who lived alone.

Scientists believe that the warming of the earth through climate change was responsible. They predict that we can expect more extreme weather in the future: more severe heat waves, cold waves, flooding, droughts, and more powerful storms.

The following year, one of the deadliest disasters in recorded history occurred on December 26, 2004. A powerful undersea earthquake, which had a magnitude of 9.1 or possibly 9.2 or 9.3—it was the third most powerful earthquake ever recorded on a seismograph—and struck off the west coast of Sumatra, Indonesia. The earthquake was so powerful that it caused the entire earth to vibrate.

The earthquake triggered a series of tsunamis that hit the coasts of all the countries bordering the Indian Ocean. Entire villages and their residents were swept away. In some places waves as high as one hundred feet swept inland spreading devastation. The hardest hit countries were Indonesia, Sri Lanka, India, and Thailand. The total death toll was more than two hundred thirty thousand people. Among the victims were many tourists and other visitors to the region from all over the world.

The next year, 2005, brought disaster to New Orleans. On August 29, Hurricane Katrina made landfall in southeastern Louisiana. Luckily, it had weakened from a Category 5 to a Category 3 hurricane. Nevertheless, Katrina was the costliest disaster in US history, as it caused $108 billion dollars in damage. There were at least 1,833 storm-related deaths. The levee system in New Orleans failed, and about 80 percent of the city was flooded. Scientists again pointed to global warming as the reason for more powerful and more frequent storms.

Mapping the Human Genome

Scientists involved in the Human Genome Project (HGP), which was launched in 1990, published the first draft of the human genome in February 2001. At that time, the sequence of the entire genome's three billion base pairs of human chromosomes was about 90 percent complete. In April 2003, the full sequence was published. The HGP scientists learned that there are about 20,500 human genes.

With the completed human genomic sequence, they could identify the location of each gene. Thanks to the HGP, we now have detailed information about the structure, organization, and function of the complete set of human genes. In other words, the basic processes controlling the development and functioning of a human being.

Looking ahead, human health will be transformed through continuing genetic research. The ability to analyze each person's genome will lead to more effective forms of preventive medicine, as well as new treatments of disease.

Pluto's Questionable Status

Pluto was discovered by astronomer Clyde Tombaugh in 1930. The ninth planet in our solar system, Pluto is the farthest planet from the sun at a distance of 3.6 billion miles. With a radius of seven hundred fifty miles, Pluto is the smallest planet, and it is Pluto's size that has thrown the planet's status into question. In January 2005, astronomer Mike Brown discovered another celestial body in Pluto's region of the solar system that is 27 percent bigger than Pluto. The new object, named 136199 Eris, is one of thousands of similar objects out beyond the orbit of Neptune, the eighth planet. These objects are classified as dwarf planets.

Now since Pluto was classified as a planet, then it would seem that Eris would also have to be so classified. After a lengthy heated debate, the International Astronomical Union in 2006 came to a decision. Size matters. Pluto was reclassified as a dwarf planet and given a minor planet designator in front of its name: 134340 Pluto.

Many people were unhappy with this decision as they had always thought of the solar system as having nine planets, which included Pluto. Debates regarding Pluto's demotion to dwarf planet status would continue into the next decade with ongoing pressure to restore Pluto's planet status.

Hurricane Katrina devastated the city of New Orleans.

Conclusion

Like any other decade, there was so much about the 2000s that was amazing. But for the most part, the decade was difficult for America—very difficult. The decade started on a high note. President Bill Clinton, who was entering his last year in office, was still very popular. The nation was at peace, and the economy was strong. But things soon started to go downhill. In March 2000, the stock market crashed, destroyed many new unprofitable dot-com companies, and wiped away many people's investments. It would take a few years for the American economy to recover from the dot-com crash.

The presidential election in November 2000 ran into trouble when disputes arose over which candidate had won the most votes in Florida. At stake were Florida's twenty-five electoral votes, which each candidate needed to win the election. The US Supreme Court declared George Bush the winner even though Al Gore had won the popular vote.

Then on September 11, 2001, the United States was attacked. Terrorists hijacked passenger planes and crashed them into New York's World Trade Center and the Pentagon. The World Trade Center was destroyed, the Pentagon badly damaged, and about three thousand people were killed. This horrific event would lead to America going to war for the rest of the decade in Afghanistan and Iraq. President Bush was determined to bring the "evildoers"—Osama bin Laden and his al-Qaeda group—to justice.

Although Americans were totally shaken by the 9/11 attacks, the nation eventually returned to normal. People went to work. People went shopping. People went to the movies. Children went to school.

And the economy eventually recovered. But it was a different kind of normal. There was now a new Department of Homeland Security, and keeping America secure from terrorists who might be lurking anywhere became the government's highest priority. Of course, things were far from normal for those men and women sent off to fight in the Middle East and for their families at home.

To help take their minds off the dangers facing the nation, Americans found relief and pleasure at the movies. A constant stream of wonderful fantasies, some taking place on other worlds, provided a perfect escape. Americans also enjoyed new ways of listening to music, thanks to the iPod, iTunes, and YouTube. And the introduction of smartphones gave people a new and exciting way to communicate.

Later in the decade, a bubble developed in the housing market caused by home prices that had risen too fast. By 2007, home prices in many cities began dropping and then proceeded to fall off a cliff. The following year, the nation was facing a total financial collapse. Millions of Americans were losing their homes, millions were losing their jobs, and there seemed to be no end in sight.

During the 2008 presidential election campaign, many Americans were drawn to Barack Obama, the Democratic candidate, who was promising to bring change. This is what people wanted to hear. Obama won the election and became the nation's first African American president. In 2009, President Obama acted quickly to prevent America's Great Recession from turning into a second Great Depression.

As the 2000s drew to a close, Americans were hopeful that Obama would end the wars in Iraq and Afghanistan. They looked forward with some optimism to an improved economy and a less dangerous world in the next decade.

Security was always on the minds of Americans throught the 2000s.

Timeline

2000 On December 12, the US Supreme Court reaches a decision in favor of George Bush in the bitterly contested presidential election between George Bush and Al Gore.

2001 In January, Apple releases iTunes. On January 20, George W. Bush is inaugurated as the 43rd president of the United States. In February, the first draft of the Human Genome Project is published. On September 11, al-Qaeda terrorists attack America and destroy New York's World Trade Center, badly damage the Pentagon, and kill about three thousand people. September 16, President Bush declares a war on terror. On September 20, Bush demands that the Taliban hand over al-Qaeda leaders. On October 7, the United States and its allies attack Afghanistan in Operation Enduring Freedom. On October 23, Steve Jobs, CEO of Apple, presents the first iPod. On October 26, the Patriot Act is signed into law by President Bush. On December 21, al-Qaeda member Richard Reid is caught trying to detonate an explosive in his shoe aboard a flight from Paris to Miami.

2002 In January, a detention center for prisoners in the war on terror is established at the Guantanamo Naval Base in Cuba. Osama bin Laden sends a letter to America listing reasons for his hatred of America. Friendster, the first general social network is founded. On September 12, George Bush makes the case for an invasion of Iraq in his address to the UN Security Council. On October 16, the US Congress passes the Authorization for the Use of Military Force Against Iraq.

2003 On February 1, the Columbia space shuttle disintegrates over Texas and Louisiana. On February 13, Secretary of State Colin Powell addresses the UN General Assembly seeking to gain authorization for an invasion of Iraq. On March 17, Bush demands that Saddam Hussein surrender and leave Iraq with his two sons within forty-eight hours. On March 18, the United States begins bombing Baghdad. On March 20, Bush announces the start of the Iraq War. On April 9, Baghdad comes under US control. In April, the completed human genetic sequence of the Human Genome Project is published. On May 1, President Bush lands on the aircraft carrier Abraham Lincoln to announce "Mission Accomplished."

2004 In April, news spreads of the torture of Iraqi prisoners by American guards at the Abu Ghraib prison. On July 27,

Barack Obama delivers the keynote address at the Democratic National Convention. In November, Obama is elected as the US Senator from Illinois. On December 26, a 9.1 earthquake off the west coast of Sumatra, Indonesia, causes a series of tsunamis that kill more than 230,000 people in the countries bordering the Indian Ocean. The deadly terrorist bombings of commuter trains takes place in Madrid. Mark Zuckerberg creates Facebook.

2005 In January, astronomer Mike Brown discovers the dwarf planet Eris. On January 30, a presidential election is held in Iraq. In July, terrorists bomb underground lines and bus routes in London. On August 29, Hurricane Katrina causes devastating flooding of New Orleans, kills 1,833 people, and causes $108 billion in damage. On December 15, Iraqis elect a Parliament to a four-year term.

2006 In 2006, Pluto is reclassified as a dwarf planet by the International Astronomical Union. In April, Nuri-al-Maliki becomes the leader of Iraq's first full-term government since the fall of Saddam Hussein. On June 8, the FDA approves the use of Gardasil, an HPV vaccine, for females and males ages nine through twenty-six. Twitter is created and enables users to send and read short 140-character messages called "tweets."

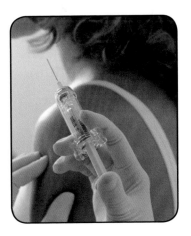

2007 Home prices begin dropping. Apple releases the iPhone. Barry Bonds breaks Hank Aaron's home run record. Amazon releases the Kindle e-reader.

2008 On June 7, Senator Hillary Clinton concedes the race for the Democratic nomination for president to Barack Obama. On June 23, Obama chooses Senator Joe Biden as his running mate. American swimmer Michael Phelps wins eight gold medals at the 2008 summer Olympics in Beijing. Jamaican sprinter Usain Bolt wins three gold medals at the summer Olympics in Beijing. On November 4, Barack Obama wins the election and becomes America's first African American president. On November 17, the Iraqi Parliament ratifies a status of forces agreement with the United States.

2009 On January 20, Barack Obama is inaugurated as the 44th president of the United States. On February 17, the American Recovery and Reinvestment Act of 2009—the Stimulus—is signed into law by President Obama. On June 25, Michael Jackson dies of cardiac arrest at the age of fifty. On December 25, Uman Abdulmutallab tries to detonate plastic explosives in his underwear aboard a flight from Amsterdam to Detroit. Facebook has 150 million users, and each user has an average of more than one hundred Facebook friends.

Glossary

anthrax—A disease that is often fatal caused by the bacterium *Bacillus anthracis*.

bankruptcy—A legally declared condition when a person or organization cannot pay its debts.

bureaucracy—The body of officials and administrators, especially of a government or government department.

coalition—An alliance, especially a temporary one, between persons, groups, or nations.

electoral vote—The vote cast in the electoral college of the United States by the representative of each state in a presidential election.

hijack—To seize control of a vehicle or airplane in transit.

inaugurated—Inducted into office with formal ceremonies.

infrastructure—The underlying systems that allow something to function.

jihad—A war against nonbelievers waged by Muslims.

mortgage—A loan agreement in which the borrower offers the purchased property as security or guarantee of repayment to the lender.

mujahideen—Muslim guerilla fighters, especially in Afghanistan.

recession—A period of economic contraction.

social media—Web sites used by large groups of people to share information and to develop social and professional contacts.

surveillance—Continuous observation of a place, person, group, or ongoing activity in order to gather information.

terrorist—A person who uses violence and threats to spread fear and make political statements.

Further Reading

Books

Benoit, Peter. *September 11: We Will Never Forget*. New York, N.Y.: Children's Press, 2012.

Doak, Robin S. *Homeland Security*. New York, N.Y.: Scholastic Inc., 2012.

Ellis, Deborah. *Children of War: Voices of Iraqi Refugees*. Toronto, Ontario: Groundwood Books, 2010.

Friedman, Mark. *America's Struggles with Terrorism*. New York, N.Y.: Scholastic Inc., 2012.

Heinrichs, Ann. *The Great Recession*. New York, N.Y.: Scholastic Inc., 2012.

Hollander, Barbara. *Booms, Bubbles, and Busts: The Economic Cycle*. Chicago, Ill.: Heinemann Library, 2011.

Sterngass, Jon. *Terrorism*. Tarrytown, New York, N.Y.: Marshall Cavendish Corporation, 2012.

Zeiger, Jennifer. *The War in Afghanistan*. New York, N.Y.: Children's Press, 2012.

Web Sites

dhs.gov
> Read all about the Department of Homeland Security, a federal government division that was formed after the 9/11 attacks to protect the nation from terrorists.

stateofworkingamerica.org/great-recession/
> Read how the US labor market was affected by the worst recession since the Great Depression of the 1930s.

nationalgeographic.com/remembering-9-11/
> View photos, hear recordings from the passengers aboard the hijacked planes, and explore survivor mementos on National Geographic's *Remembering 9/11* Web site.

Movies

The Impossible. Directed by J. A. Bayona. Burbank, Calif.: Warner Brothers, 2012.
> This movie depicts the true story of a family that endured the 2004 Indian Ocean Tsunami.

United 93. Directed by Paul Greengrass. Universal City, Calif.: Universal Pictures, 2006.
> This film dramatizes the events of the hijacked plane that crashed in a Pennsylvania field on September 11, 2001.

Index

Pluto, 82
Powell, Colin, 60
presidential election, 52, 60, 63, 67, 84, 85

Q

Queen Elizabeth II, 36
Quran, 64

R

Ramon, Ilan, 74
reality TV, 32, 33, 35
Rehabilitation Institute of Chicago, 76
Reid, Richard, 20
Republican Party, 52, 60, 68, 69
Russia, 61, 70, 73

S

Saudi Arabia, 14
Schrader, Ken, 46
September 11, 2001 (9/11), 7, 10, 17, 18, 35, 41, 60, 65, 75, 84
Shia, 63, 64
Shock and Awe, 62
smartphones, 36, 73
social media, 24, 28
Soetoro, Lolo, 65
Soviets, 55, 56
Spears, Britney, 39
Star Trek, 42
Star Wars, 42
Stevens, Bob, 17
stock market, 20, 84
student loans, 22
Sullivan, Jesse, 76
summer Olympics, 46, 51
Sumatra, 80
Sunni, 63, 64

T

Tajiks, 56
Talib, Ali Ibn Abi, 64
Taliban, 17, 56, 59
Taylor, Elizabeth, 40
Tikrit, 63
Timberlake, Justin, 39
Tito, Dennis, 70
Tombaugh, Clyde, 82
Tora Bora Mountains, 56

Transportation Security Administration (TSA), 18, 20
Tsunami, 80
Twin Towers, 10, 13, 14
Twitter, 27, 28

U

Ugg Boots, 27
Underwood, Carrie, 39
unemployment rate, 22
United Nations, 59, 60
UN Security Council, 59, 61
UN weapons inspectors, 59, 60
USA PATRIOT Act, 7, 21
US Congress, 59, 61, 65
US Senate, 61
US Supreme Court, 52, 55, 84
Uzbeks, 56

W

weapons of mass destruction (WMDs), 7, 59, 60, 62
West, Kanye, 39
White House, 13, 36
World Trade Center, 10, 13, 14, 75, 84

Y

YouTube, 36, 85
Y2K transition, 6

Z

Zuckerberg, Mark, 24